Domestic Vic

YOUR RELATIONSHIP

COURSE 1

Written by Melanie Survivor

www.melaniesurvivor.com

DOMESTIC VIOLENCE – YOUR RELATIONSHIP – Course 1

Author: Melanie Survivor

www.melaniesurvivor.com

Facebook: Melanie Survivor

ISBN 978-0-6485160-0-2

 NATIONAL LIBRARY OF AUSTRALIA

A catalogue record for this book is available from the National Library of Australia

Dedications

I dedicate this course to all the people who feel lost in their relationships. My aim is to help you with the first step that is easy and accessible to find your way to happiness.

Acknowledgements

I have been so blessed to work with so many amazing clients over the years.

Some of my clients have suggested I write books, in relation to the different relationship issues couples and families face, because I empowered and inspired them. Something that is easy to read and provides exercises to complete, by themselves or with their partner in the comfort of their own home. A first step before counselling and to assist with counselling.

The client's that have suggested this are the ones trying to fix their relationship and their partner will not attend counselling with them. Their relationship ends before it's had a chance to be worked on, most partners saying we don't need a third party, we can work through this ourselves.

They say if there was something out there as a first step, they may-be would be able to help their relationship and help their partner become more aware and understanding of counselling and even maybe want to attend counselling.

I have listened and heard my client's and have commenced creating on line relationship courses, (you can also purchase in hard copy).

My aim in creating the courses, is as a first step for everyone who wants to try to fix their relationships. I share knowledge gained from my education, expertise and personal experience, I share stories and provide exercises to complete. Helping them to become more aware of their situation and choices.

When I planned my online courses, my analogy was like tying a shoe lace, if you miss a step when tying a shoe lace, you're shoe lace may not be tied.

The same as if you miss or skip a critical part of the course you may not get the safe and effective outcome that you desire.

I thank all my clients who inspired me and wish them every happiness.

I believe it takes a village to help rid the world of domestic violence and I never profess to have all the information or all the answers.

The village I refer to is the professionals, who are recommended at the end of each course should further assistance be required. My colleagues the therapists, counsellors, psychologists, lawyers, police officers, paramedics I thank you and if I haven't met you, I am always available to meet a new friend.

I appreciate and have sourced information and photos for this course from different arenas. I have not listed every arena separately.

I wish to provide a blanket thank you to all sources I have utilised to help create this course for domestic violence victims.

Contents

Disclaimer

The material in this course is for general education and information and is intended as a guide only.

It is not intended to replace professional counselling, nor is it intended to provide comprehensive information on issues that might arise in human relationships. No person or organisation should act on the basis of the information in this course without taking appropriate advice.

The situations I share in this course are true and correct, genuine and honest recollections of my relationship journeys or client's journeys.

The content of this course is liable to change, and although we attempt to ensure that it is current and accurate, we do not guarantee its currency as there may be delays, errors or omissions.

Melanie Survivor reserves the right to make modifications of any nature to the information, without update.

Course Overview

Welcome, I understand how hard it is for you to take this first step to find out why you are feeling uncertain in your relationship.

You probably don't hear this a lot, "I am so proud of you". This is the first step to taking control of your own life/the life of your children and your relationship.

I also understand deep down inside you may not want to believe your relationship is in that much trouble. You just know something isn't right and you want to fix it.

Depending on how long you have been in your relationship. Depending on the severity of the situation that has made you feel uncertain or whether you are living in a domestic violence relationship, as you progress through this course, you may become extremely angry or emotional and upset with yourself or your partner.

If this happens please note it is a totally normal response. If you are unable to control your anger, I ask you seek assistance. You can find organisations in Module 8 of this course that will be able to help you.

Working on yourself and your relationship when you are emotional is never going to be easy.

You may want to give up, you may say it's a load of rubbish because it pushes buttons, takes you from a comfort zone, even if that comfort zone is unhealthy and causes you discomfort.

If this happens take some time out and return to the course when you feel you can, but can I please empower you not to give up and to understand you are worthy of happiness.

If you feel the need to just put up with it, that unknown feeling that something is wrong, may-be thinking, better the devil you know, right! The grass is always greener on the other side right! ACTUALLY WRONG.

I suggest taking this time out to read my book, "Surviving the Devil, Escaping Domestic Violence, a True Story". I only say this not to sell my book because that is not why I am here, but I have been told it will help you understand, provides you with a different perspective so you can make an informed choice.

I have lived in a domestic violence relationship; my story may help you with your journey as I have been told it has helped others.

I am living proof that there is an amazing life waiting for you, and I do understand you need to be ready. I also understand the first time you leave a domestic violence relationship is not always the last time you leave that relationship. If I could back and tell my young self some wisdom, it would be to be kind to yourself and keep safe.

I have created my relationship courses as your first step, for you to gain knowledge and understand you have choices, one being a change towards happiness in your life.

I wanted to provide you with some tools I didn't have when I felt lost and alone. I didn't seek counselling, I couldn't seek counselling, if he found out? I knew my relationship wasn't right, but I didn't think it was that bad, because I didn't know I was being brain washed by the narcissist and his family and I didn't remember what a healthy relationship looked like.

I felt there was nowhere to turn back then. If would have loved any of the Melanie Survivor courses, something I could gain knowledge from, from someone who had experienced similar feelings to me, lived in a domestic violence relationship.

A course that was simple and easy, no stress, no pressure and no judgment. A course I could complete in my own time at my own pace, anywhere I was, I would have bought them.

I wanted to make the courses as assessible and as affordable as possible for you.

Module 7 provides tools that may help you if you start to feel uneasy. At any time refer to those tools and if they do not help in module 8, I have added the list of services that may help. (Note: services are in Australia, Outside Australia google domestic violence services near you)

This course has been created firstly to help you ascertain some initial ideas, knowledge and understanding of what is wrong with your relationship and to help you confirm if you are living in a domestic violence or unhealthy relationship. This course provides you with insight to what a healthy relationship looks like and what you should require in your relationship. It also provides you with some tools and knowledge on how to build your boundaries that work for you.

Maybe your fighting the internal battle of "I love him, why can't he just love me the way I deserve to be loved?" or "I love him, I can help him be a better man" or "I just love him, I couldn't leave him"

During this course, you will be working through issues that have arisen or may arise, remember not all the issues I share may relate to your situation, the course covers a myriad of situations that may occur.

I will be sharing with you during each module the situation presented for that module, providing you with varied examples I have personally experienced or have been shared by my clients, with their permission of course.

Some modules will be "read only" providing you with information and some modules will have exercises for you to complete and provide feedback. As advised above additional tools are also provided in module 7, if at any time you feel emotionally drained. I know I repeat myself, I care and want to make sure you are ok during this process as best I can?

Please note this was a difficult course to create due to my knowledge that all individuals have a past, react differently, are emotional beings and what works, for one family (family meaning a couple, heterosexual or same sex with or without children); may not work for all families. Your family is special to you, different from any other.

My intention is that you take from the course the information and tools that work for you and please know there is no right or wrong answers and definitely no silly answers.

Work through this course at your own time, in safety and at your own pace. There is no time limit to when you finish the course, this is totally up to you.

Before we begin, may I suggest prior to commencing each module you find a quiet place where you will not be interrupted?

If you have children, I suggest waiting until they go to bed or are at school or at a friend/family's place. This is very important for each module, so you can really concentrate with a clear uninterrupted mind.

Read each question and answer honestly from your heart. It is most important to be raw and honest with yourself, for this process to work! Take your time.

Unfortunately, depending on your situation some memories that arise, may be daunting. Allow yourself the time and emotional support to detach!

Remember we are all human and we all make choices! You made a choice to be in a relationship, if a relationship doesn't work or is unhealthy, you have a choice to stay or go?

If you find a question upsets you, it may be because it has hit a nerve, down deep. Cry if you need to, it is part of the cleansing process. Remember Module 7 and Module 8.

May I suggest not moving from one module to the next until you feel you have completed that section.

The course is designed to move from one step to the next and jumping modules may create confusion.

If after completing the course and depending on your individual relationship, you may want to work through the course with your partner, or:

If you feel you need additional help, please refer to module 8, Helpful Services, which provides a list of organisations that may be of assistance or google domestic violence counsellors or if you don't feel you are living in domestic violence, then marriage counsellors in your area.

NOTE: When attending a counsellor/therapist, or domestic violence organisation, provide a copy of this course with your answers, this will help them understand where you are at and how you are currently feeling, and save you money on obtaining the initial information we all require as therapists. This course is also created to help therapists, counsellors, psychologists, to help you.

Domestic Violence – Escaping Domestic Violence Course 2 provides you with the understanding of stay or go and the knowledge and tools to help you leave as safely as possible, should you wish to gain knowledge of the above you can locate the course at www.melaniesurvivor.com

Let's begin Course 1:

MODULE ONE:
About the Creator

Hi, my name is Mel and I know now all my life relationship experiences have led me to you, to assist and serve you, by sharing information through true stories, life experiences and relationship courses you can complete on line.

At the beginning of each module I will share with you stories relative to that module.

You too can change your world, become the survivor that rests and hides inside of you. I can say this because no matter what was thrown at me, I am and will always be a survivor, my choice.

I didn't realise at the time that every rotten, negative, abusive experience was providing me with the tools and knowledge to really help you!

Learn from my mistakes, it doesn't mean you won't make your own because we are all human, what I provide you with is information and knowledge to use however it suits you. I give you the opportunity to make informed choices.

Knowledge is power and by sharing I hope you find your inner power, your inner strength and your self-love.

I share my first domestic violence relationship in my book "Surviving the Devil, Escaping Domestic Violence", A True Story. I was tired and scared, holding down a full-time job, bringing up and protecting my daughter and surviving and hiding from the Devil and his family, it was really exhausting. (I was engaged to but did not marry the Devil).

If you have not read the book, I suggest we pause here as reading the book will give you so much insight. You can purchase the book from www.melaniesurvivor.com, www.amazon.com, www.barnesandnoble.com and many more. I have been told it is an easy read, inspiring, empowering and has helped readers in their relationship. For example - a lady told me after reading the book she felt so blessed to be with her husband and she stopped taking him for granted, their relationship blossomed, another lady didn't realise how bad her marriage was, she had been living with an alcoholic for nearly 20 years and my book gave her the power to leave and leave safely and break the cycle.

Years after escaping the Devil, I met a wonderful man whom I married, I will call him my first husband. I thought I was ready to move on, obviously I wasn't, I did not look at the bigger picture, no one talked about domestic violence or what to expect how to try and work on yourself.   I still didn't love myself enough and I attracted another abuser into my life.

His true personality slowly arose, initially I never noticed as we were so wrapped up dodging the past, the Devil had returned and was now threatening both of us.

He wasn't the man he presented to me, my saviour, a man I envisaged spending the rest of my life with. Turned out he was a loner, very anti-social, negative, manipulative and controlling with narcissist tendencies and a gambler.

My first husband did not hit me however like I said he was an emotional and financial abuser.

One night I looked at him in awe and said, "I am so lucky to be with you, you treat me so well!"

His reply "No I don't, I just don't treat you as bad as the devil did, it's not hard."

The relationship was destined to fail, I am an empath, introverted but social and extremely positive. I didn't realise I was walking into a minefield of emotionally painful experiences, each step creating another atomic reaction.

I wanted to believe in that relationship and our new family. I didn't want to feel like a failure again, after all I had escaped a violent relationship, at least he didn't hit me. At the time emotional and financial abuse was not spoken of as abuse.

NO ONE spoke the raw truth "abuse is abuse and comes in many forms", I had no idea at the time.

Remember, knowledge is power.

After divorcing my first husband, I spent a lot of time working on myself, I didn't date for the longest time and when I did, I feel I must apologise to the first couple of men, because I was testing my knowledge, confirming my self-confidence, not ego and really learning to love myself. I knew my requirements and had set my boundaries, I was a different woman.

Today I live with my current husband, we have been together over a decade and live in a normal happy step relationship, we each have our say. We survived the teenage step family sagas, ex-partners interference and the past ghosts.

I am proof, you have choices, I could have stayed with any of my ex's, that was a choice, I knew I would not be happy. I knew I didn't want my girls growing up thinking that is how a male can treat them.

If you have purchased this course, I know you may be hurting and seeking tools to help your relationship survive or may-be just interested in learning different tools because some section of your relationship is not working.

Think of me as your big sister or mentor teaching you lessons, I have learnt so you don't have to make the same mistakes. Remember you deserve to be happy and you make the choices for your life, no one else.

Good luck and if at any time you feel you are in danger for your life or your children's life, immediately phone the Police in your area:

Australia 000   America 911   England 999

Just to name a few phone numbers. May I suggest that you always know wherever you are in the world the contact details of the local police and keep them close.

MODULE TWO:
What is Domestic Violence?

Domestic violence comes in many forms - psychological, emotional, physical, sexual and financial.

Acknowledging the signs of an abusive relationship is the first step to ending the pattern, taking back your self-esteem and self-worth and breaking the generational cycle.

No one should ever think they need to live in fear of the person they feel they love.

In this module, I provide you with explanations of what each form relates to providing you with awareness and knowledge.

Psychological Abuse: can be any of the following but not limited to:

- Behaviour and/or comments to undermine your sense of self

- name-calling or putdowns

- intimidation

- threatening to withhold money, is in total control of money

- sulking

- disconnecting the telephone

- taking the car away

- lying to your friends and family about you (creating distance or a void)

- telling you that you have no choice in any decisions

- Making all big decisions without consulting you

- threatening to commit suicide in general especially when you try to leave

- threatening to take your children

- threatening to report you to welfare agencies unless you do what he/she says

Does this abuse relate to your relationship? Write down your thoughts? The list above has space between each point so you can write down your own examples.

Verbal Abuse: can be any of the following not limited to:

- constant put-downs

- telling you to lose weight

- telling you, you need to change the way you dress

- calling you names

- yelling and swearing at you, you can't do anything right

- making harassing or threatening phone calls, texts or private messages

- says things to scare you (example - told or telling you something "bad" would/will happen; threatened/threatens to commit suicide if you leave)

- Using the children to threaten you (example - told or telling you, you will never get custody; threatens he will leave town with the children and you will never see them)

Does this abuse relate to your relationship? Write down your thoughts, make a list? The list above has space between each point so you can write down your own examples.

Physical Abuse: can be any of the following but not limited to:

• Actual or threatened physical harm for example:

- Injured you by causing bruises
- Injured you by cutting you

- Injured by breaking your bones

- Injured by slapping you

- Injured by punching you

- Injured by pushing you

- Injured by choking you

- Being threatened or injured with objects/weapons

- Destroying or damaging property.

• Making threats to hurt you and/or your children

• Denies you sleep, warmth or nutrition

• Denies you medical care

• Driving recklessly while you and/or your children are in the car etc

Does this abuse relate to your relationship? Write down your thoughts, make a list? The list above has space between each point so you can write down your own examples.

Social Abuse: can be any of the following but not limited to:

- Controlling where you go for example, you may be allowed to go to work and then have to return home immediately when you are finished

- Controlling who you see

- Controlling what you wear

- Keeping you from contacting family or friends

- Preventing someone from leaving the house

- Preventing someone from going to a place of worship or praying

- Making all the 'big' decisions without consultation with you

- Listens to your phone calls

- Checks the speedometer in your car and controls when you can use the car

- Calls you repeatedly at work

- Refuses to help with housework (Not just lazy)

- Refuses to look after and provide care for the children

- Make you feel guilty about going to work or socialising

- Controls your use of mobile phones

- Controls your use of phones

- Controls your use of internet

- Constantly checking up on your whereabouts etc

Does this abuse relate to your relationship? Write down your thoughts, make a list? The list above has space between each point so you can write down your own examples.

Sexual Abuse: can be any of the following but not limited to:

- Any forced or unwanted sexual contact/activity

- Pressures you to have sex when you didn't want to (will not take no for an answer)

- Forcing you to have sex or to do sexual acts you do not want or like

- Raping you

- Humiliation can often play a part in sexual abuse

- Puts you down about your sex life

NOTE: Forcing you to have sex is called rape and it is a criminal offence, even if you are married

Does this abuse relate to your relationship? Write down your thoughts, make a list? The list above has space between each point so you can write down your own examples.

Reproductive control: can be any of the following but not limited to:

This has links with sexual abuse, but is uniquely related to women's (particularly young women's) ability to control their own reproductive health, for example:

- Use or non-use of contraception/ contraceptive method

- Forcing you to make decisions around pregnancy and/or termination

- Having little say in the number and timing of your children.

Does this abuse relate to your relationship? Write down your thoughts, make a list? The list above has space between each point so you can write down your own examples.

Financial Abuse: can be any of the following but not limited to:

- Your partner takes control of the financial affairs when you don't want him to, it is not a joint decision

- Prevents you from having access to money

- Denying access to bank accounts

- Forcing the surrender of bankcards and credit cards to gain control of your income

- Preventing you from seeking or maintaining employment

- Making you ask for money for basic items such as food, petrol and clothing, and forcing you to provide receipts to account for your spending

- Refusing to give someone enough money to live on and provide for your family.

Does this abuse relate to your relationship? Write down your thoughts, make a list? The list above has space between each point so you can write down your own examples.

Property Damage: can be any of the following but not limited to:

- Kicking a hole/holes in the wall

- Scratching or breaking certain parts of your car

- Taking away or breaking things that are important to you

- Abusing a family pet

Does this abuse relate to your relationship? Write down your thoughts, make a list? The list above has space between each point so you can write down your own examples.

Stalking: can be any of the following but not limited to:

Stalking is behaviour intended to harass, intimidate and torment another person. Stalking includes a range of behaviours such as:

- Repeated phone calls

- Sending harassing letters or e-mails

- Using social media (such as signing into your Facebook or twitter accounts, ghosting your accounts)

- Loitering near your residence or place of work

- Spying on or openly watching you

- Following you, whenever you are, he/she just appears out of no where

- Harming pets

- Organizing unwanted home deliveries

- Sending flowers, chocolates, cards, presents

- Damaging your property

- Moving your belongings around

- Changing details on personal identification

Does this abuse relate to your relationship? Write down your thoughts, make a list? The list above has space between each point so you can write down your own examples.

Technological abuse – can be the following but not limited to:

This is an emerging form of abuse that is linked to stalking, psychological abuse and other forms of domestic violence. It can mean that technology is used to directly or indirectly monitor and stalk you.

This can occur without your knowledge so be careful.

- Posting your personal information on websites

- Tracking devices being installed in cars

- Tracking devise being installed on your mobile phones
    o GPS
    o Spyware
    o Listening devices
    o Hidden cameras
    o Keystroke-logging hardware

Does this abuse relate to your relationship? Write down your thoughts, make a list? The list above has space between each point so you can write down your own examples.

How did you go?

If you have written examples next to the majority of the above, you may be residing in domestic violence. If you feel you are in danger phone the police immediately.

Healthy relationships do not obtain the above traits. They may contain snippets if not physically abusive, and your partner agrees, you may be able to work on those traits together to rid them from your relationship.

For example: You may call each other names and speak derogatory to each other, with help you will be able to stop such speak, which we know at times can be hurtful.

Module 3 "The Quiz" is to help you ascertain whether your relationship is just going through a rough patch or you are living in domestic violence.

MODULE THREE:
The Quiz - Am I living in Domestic Violence?

If you recognise that you or someone you know may be living in domestic violence, may I suggest taking this quiz!

I know the scariest part of any relationship is when you realise that you are not living as a loving couple/family; your connection is from manipulation and the need for your partner to control you, not from unconditional love.

Even though that is what an abuser would like you to believe - that they love you - reality is they need to control you and their version is not a healthy version of love.

Do you continue fighting that feeling that your relationship doesn't feel right to you? Maybe you don't want to acknowledge it as you may-be scared of change, especially when living in domestic violence.

Are you holding on to the hope that your relationship will get better, is that what you want to believe? You don't want to acknowledge that you have been brainwashed and manipulated into this relationship of abuse.

It doesn't matter if you are living in a normal or abusive relationship; the realisation of a possible ending in any form of relationship is difficult to come to terms with and let's face it, also very emotional.

Sometimes a break up is inevitable - all your fears, all those doubts that have been dancing around in your head saying this is not right, you deserve better, your intuition screaming at you that you are not safe, all that negative self-talk blaming yourself for your situation is a reality.

Know it is an injustice to you and your family to stay living in abuse.

It will take a village to help break the cycle of abuse, but it can start now, it can start with you. Know you are not alone, reach out and let others help you break the cycle of abuse - let's help you find your voice.

Domestic abuse often gets worse the longer you stay in the abusive relationship and the more control and manipulation your abuser has over you.

He/she has charmed their way into your heart, once he/she knows they have captured you, their true colours start to present and before you know it you are being controlled, they often begin with threats, financial and verbal abuse which can escalate to physical violence, rape and sometimes death.

Whilst it is easier to know you are in a physically or sexually abusive relationship, the emotional and psychological consequences of domestic abuse are also severe and soul destroying.

Emotional abuse although harder to detect, destroys your self-worth, can lead to anxiety and depression and makes you feel helpless and alone, you may feel you are not worthy of real love and this type of abuse builds "I am not good enough" persona. You might feel that no one would understand because there are no physical scars. Believe me they will.

A real loving healthy relationship between two people does not offer any kind of abuse and this type of relationship does exist and is obtainable to you.

The most obvious of all the signs of living in a domestic violence relationship is a feeling of fear of your partner. For example, walking on eggshells around your partner, or losing who you truly are inside, by becoming passive and not speaking your words in fear of either a verbal or physical reprisal.

Your first step to finding yourself again, the true you are recognising that your situation is abusive. You start by answering the quiz questions below, with a truly honest and open heart. If you find yourself making excuses for your partner you may not be answering the quiz honestly.

Find a quiet place to work through the questions without interruption. Grab yourself a coffee/tea and give yourself some time.

The more times you answer "yes", the more likely it is that you are living in an abusive relationship.

FORMS OF ABUSE – (This quiz uses the word "partner", but keep in mind your abuser can be your spouse, romantic partner, a family member, or anyone else that does these things to you.	YES/NO
Do you feel . . .	
Afraid of your partner most of the time?	
You can't do anything right for your partner?	
Fear to say what you feel in case you upset or outrage your partner?	
Emotionally numb and helpless?	
You may be the crazy one as everything is always your fault?	
Believe it is your fault you are being hurt or mistreated?	
Does your partner . . . ?	
Humiliate or yell at you?	
Blame you for their own abusive behaviour?	
Ignore you or put your opinions or accomplishments down?	
See you as their property or a sex object, rather than a person?	
Treat you so badly that you're embarrassed for your friends or family to see?	
Criticize you and put you down?	
Destroy your belongings?	
Force you to have sex? (This is rape 'no always means no'.)	
Hurt you, or threaten to hurt or kill you?	
Have a bad and unpredictable temper?	
Threaten to take your children away or harm them?	
Threaten to commit suicide if you leave him?	
Act excessively jealous and possessive? This is not love.	
Try to control where you go or what you do?	
Stop or distance you from seeing your friends and family?	
Constantly check up on you?	
Limit your access to money, a phone or the car?	
Gamble excessively?	
Drink or take drugs excessively, or exhibit changes in behaviour?	
Lead their own life, making you feel like you just slot in? (When you raise this they make it all your fault, they need time out etc.)	

How are you feeling? The more you answered yes to a question in the Quiz, the more likely it is you are residing in a domestic violence situation.

Breath, try and stay calm, now is not the time to react but respond to what you have acknowledged.

If you feel you need to obtain professional advice, refer to module 8, or google domestic violence helpline in your area.

If you are feeling ok, continue at your own pace through the rest of this course, it is enlightening to what fears are, what your relationship requirements should be and gives you the tools to set boundaries.

If you feel the need to leave, I have created a course *Escaping Domestic Violence – Action Plan Course 2*, which provides tools and suggestions on how to leave safely, helping you build your flexible action plan to a better life.

Keep safe and whatever you do, right now it will be beneficial to become the chameleon, I was once. What that means is your partner cannot find out you are looking at choices to stay or go?

Also, now would be a good time to tell a family member, a friend, a counsellor (Important: someone you can trust), that you feel you may be living in domestic violence situation. You will understand in more detail why this is so important when completing Course 2, Escaping Domestic Violence – Action Plan.

MODULE FOUR:
Is FEAR holding you back?

All of us experience fear now and then. And all of us know the effects fear can have on us. Fear can hold us back from pursuing our dreams, like leaving in an unhealthy or abusive relationship. It can keep us stuck where we are.

If fear is keeping you from being who you want to be or what you want to accomplish, start by understanding what your fear means.

In this module I ask you to read the different sources of fear, acknowledge if this type of fear is holding you back and write down real life experiences. Let's begin:

Here are six common sources.

1. FEAR - For Everything a Reason

Fear isn't always bad, of course. It keeps us from doing lots of things that are dumb and dangerous. But the kind of fear that gets between you and the things you want often disguises itself as reasonable caution. To understand the difference, ask yourself what's on the other side of your fear. If it's something with little payoff besides risk-taking, it's likely the wiser path is to listen to your fear. But if the fear is holding you back from something significant you want - especially if it's a significant change in your life - it's time to fight.

Can you relate to this type of fear?

2. FEAR - Face Everything and Recover

Fear frequently rears up when we begin to gain a level of understanding about our lives. Recovery - whether it's from a past event or a present obstacle - is one of the greatest gifts you can give yourself, but it's natural for a part of you to prefer the comfort of the current situation. If you're thinking through something serious in your life and everything locks up, that's fear trying to take charge, be wise, think the situation through and don't let fear get the best of you.

Can you relate to this type of fear?

3. FEAR - Find Excuses and Reasons

When we try something new, there's almost always a period of uncertainty and discomfort. It's at exactly that point that fear kicks in and pushes us back to safe ground. If this pattern develops long enough, eventually we don't even consider change but go straight to the reasons why it won't work. It's your choice: you can either allow your world to shrink because you've been paralysed by fear and negativity, or just commit to taking the next step and watching the world start to open up.

Can you relate to this type of fear?

4. FEAR - Frantic Effort to Avoid Reality

Fear takes us away from what we know and tries to lure us into a kind of alternate reality - one that rewards us for timidity, for staying quiet and staying put, for settling. Of course, we know those things aren't true. Rewards come to those who jump in and take chances. Sometimes you have to shove fear aside to stay grounded in the real world.

Can you relate to this type of fear?

5. FEAR - False Evidence Appearing Real

Danger is real; fear, on the other hand, is a product of our thoughts. We create it, and ultimately, we give or deny it power. Fear can sure feel like reality. You overcome it when you remember you are strong because you know your weaknesses, you are powerful because you know your flaws, and you are determined because you know reality from fear's falsehood.

Can you relate to this type of fear?

6. FEAR - Forget Everything and Run

There's no denying the temptation: when things turn tough, the easiest way through is to turn and run. But that's not the path to achievement and success. If you can find the courage to stand your ground, you hold the power.

Fear shows up in lots of different forms, but the only way out is through - staying present in the moment and committed to the things you want to accomplish. It's your life you're standing up for. See it as an adventure. Feel the fear and do it anyway and watch your life blossom.

Can you relate to this type of fear?

OK, are you ready, found your quiet place?

Let's start:-

Write down your inner fears as you have acknowledged above in relation to your relationship, in point form.

Remember write down your true feelings for each question, it is most important to be raw and honest!

No one will see this but you and in time maybe a domestic violence counsellor. Remember you are never alone, there is so much help out there now for you.

Now you have written down your fears, understand you can add or delete as your progress through the course and your understanding and knowledge increases, it may change how you think about your fears. Next is to write down the reasons beside each fear and examples why this fear has trapped you in your situation?

For example: One of my fears was will he hurt or kidnap my daughter if I leave? *Reason for fear:* The Devil had threatened this on occasions (I suggest writing the dates and times if you remember, this assists in future if you require a Protective or Domestic Violence Order) and the unknown scared me.

OR: A client's fear was "How will I bring the kids up on my own?" *Reason for fear*: Lack of knowledge. She attended an appointment and was provided with the understanding, knowledge and tools she required. Her fear disappeared.

NOTE: This process is helpful information should you need to obtain a Protective or Domestic Violence order.

Use this page to write your answers, list your fear then write your example

MODULE FIVE: Your REQUIREMENTS for your Relationship

Abusive, unhealthy, manipulative, controlling, toxic, critical, negative, damaging

They are NOT words, I associate with healthy relationships.

I was that woman, the one living in an unhealthy relationship and not knowing it. I was manipulated into a field of destruction, abuse and a very unhealthy relationship. I made the same mistakes over and over again as I tried to claw my way out, lost and confused.

The Devil (my abuser) had created a fear inside of me that was debilitating, and I did not understand that I had a choice, that I owned my life no one else had the right to control me, that I was making the choice to stay.

We all have a choice and not all choices are fun and exciting some are hard, confusing and confrontational, but they are ours to make.

When I gained my internal strength, my self-confidence I realised I had the ability to make my own choices and I made the right one for me, I created a plan and I escaped.

When I searched deep inside my heart and soul and finally listened to my intuition, I understood that I was not living in a healthy relationship. I realised I didn't even know what a healthy relationship looked like, so how could I know how to live in one.

After years of abuse, my view was so tainted on relationships. Wasn't I supposed to be soft and accommodating, not rock the boat, keep the man happy and pacify any situation so not to be punished for not understanding! Didn't I realise I was the cause for any fights and disruptions in our relationship, if only I would just listen to him. I had learnt how to survive and to be honest with you I become emotionally closed off without realising I had lost myself.

My first step was learning to love me more than my partner, this is called self-love.

It isn't easy depending on how much damage has been created and for how long you have been treated badly, however you can re-program your thinking, you can still be kind and giving but strong and powerful. You have the inner strength to be truly happy.

I researched everything, read every book, attended courses, learned to meditate, the power of being grateful and the power of daily affirmations.

Once I achieved this knowledge and started to believe in myself, my inner strength, inner power and my self-worth increased.

I chose to be alone during this part of my journey as I did not want to be distracted and I did not want to attract another broken person, who I would feel compelled to help see the light and who would drag me into the darkness.

There is no time limit on how long this process takes, we are individuals and we need all have our own pace.

When I was ready, I began dating. I noticed I was attracting a different type of man, if I saw any red flags or felt the niggly something doesn't feel right feeling inside, I had the inner strength to move on.

At this point I realised I had learned to love myself more than I loved any man. I trusted myself, was connected with my inner self and learned to listen to my intuition.

After a few different dating experiences, I met the man of my dreams and for the past 14 years have been living in a very healthy relationship.

Real love is pure, unconditional, uplifting and supportive, it makes us a better person with no expectations from our partner.

It is magical and obtainable to everyone, you just need to know the tools to help bring it out.   I believe there are five basic elements to help create a loving relationship with another person.

My question to you is are all or some of these elements present, in your current relationship? Write it down, as only you know.

1. **Self-love**
2. **Trust**
3. **Honesty**
4. **Communication**
5. **Connection**

An explanation of each element is provided below, with scenario's or questions for you to answer.

NOTE: We need all five elements in some capacity to obtain that loving HEALTHY relationship we all desire.

No. 1 - SELF LOVE

What is self-love you may be thinking?

The answer is "a regard for one's own well-being and happiness".

It is just my opinion, that self-love is the most important aspect of any good relationship.

You must learn to love yourself first.

Self-love is not demanding, manipulative, egotistical or controlling to another. It is acknowledging it is ok to set healthy boundaries for yourself.

In order to experience a loving healthy relationship, we must know what we require. Loving one-self creates a stronger capacity to love others.

It opens your heart to love without FEAR.

It makes you stronger.

A quick tool to start you on your journey to self-love is to look in the mirror everyday and say to yourself, "I love you, just the way you are?" The first time I did this I laughed so much, it felt so silly. Clearly, I did not love my self at that time. With consistency and continuing daily, my self-love grew.

When two self-loving people connect, they have the ability to experience the full aspect of love.

Scenario: You attend a party with your partner, he is handsy and flirting with all the women at the party. He is not intentionally meaning to ignore you, he is just caught up in the other women at the party. He is having an amazing time without you, even though you are right there. For you it feels like he loves the security of you, of your relationship but really loves being single because that is the way he is acting. It makes you feel, disrespected, unloved, untrusting of him.

What do you do? Circle the answer you resonate with the most or number your first answer to your least?

1. Sit in the corner and get more upset, but don't dare say anything to him for fear of his retaliation, after all isnt he allowed to have fun and aren't you just over reacting.

2. Ignore him and mingle with everyone at the party, creating your own fun, you will show him. You get totally drunk, after all he is just being him and even though it bothers you now, you hope he will change in the future, so you don't say anything.

3. Stay away from him, cold shoulder treatment, you flirt with the males at the party, you will show him, two can play at that game and then you forgive him the next day.

4. Be polite and open at the party, have fun but don't get drunk or cause a scene. The next day at an appropriate time, you speak with him and explain to him how he makes you feel when he acts in that way.

You explain to him if that is who he is and how he wants to act, that is fine, you just need to know because you are not the woman for him.

Explaining it is his choice? (Possible outcomes he ends the relationship, it will be painful, but not as painful as living with someone who doesn't respect you)

When you are living in self-love the answer is no 4.

You don't let his behaviour ruin your evening and you don't let him get away with it either. You are not offering an ultimatum. Men hate ultimatums, they feel judged and do not think clearly plus ultimatums are controlling.

You are clearly, kindly from a place of love speaking your truth. You know deep inside he may not choose you, more importantly though you remember you chose you first. You know deep down that you could not live your life feeling those disrespectful feelings every time you go out.

Knowing yourself well enough now that if you accepted this behaviour it would create an anxiety and fear inside of you that you no longer resonate with and you are setting the precedent that this behaviour is ok.

Remember a good man who unconditionally loves you will choose you.

No 2 – TRUST

One would think, isn't this obvious?

A little secret, did you know there are a lot of people living in relationships that don't trust their partners. I know this was one of my major lessons because after escaping abuse I didn't feel worthy, I had no self-confidence as I had lived in a world of lies and deceit from my partner for so very long.

The tool here is to build your confidence and loving yourself completely before you commence a new relationship.

It is harder to work on when you are living with an abuser but not impossible.

The stronger you are as an individual, the more you take control of your own life and realise you have choices, the easier it will become to trust someone else.

If you partner is not trustworthy, I ask you **"Why are you staying?"** Write here why you feel you are staying in a non-trustworthy relationship?

If you are staying in a non-trusting relationship, you have limited self-worth, maybe you never had any self-worth, but maybe your abuser has worked his magic and knocked you down so much you don't trust yourself anymore.

He may say things like "You're crazy – that never happened?"

"Are you sure? You tend to have a bad memory?"

"It's all in your head"

"I wasn't at that party, I don't know what you are talking about, you need to get your facts right before accusing me."

I provide above a few examples of phrases your partner might say to you, that may start you questioning your own perception of reality, your own sanity, within your relationship?

The above is called "gaslighting" by mental health professionals. Once an abusive partner has broken you down your ability to trust your own thoughts and feelings disappears, you start second guessing yourself and start to believe he is right. This is just one of many tools an abuser uses to keep you in the relationship.

Answer the scenarios below, my answer is at the end of the 4th scenario.

Scenario 1: Your partner goes out all the time, more than five times per week and you are left at home by yourself or with the kids (if you have children). You have no way of going anywhere even if you wanted to as he takes the car, and if you have a spare car the keys to that car and he leaves you with no money. When he arrives home each night you smell a different fragrance of perfume then you wear, he has no money left and he is overly happy to see you.

Do you trust him or not?
Why?

Scenario 2: Your partner tells you he is going fishing with his mates. You want him to have fun and wish him a great time. When the boys arrive to pick him up for fishing, you notice they are all wearing their good going out shirts under their fishing shirts? Your partner walks out with a big overnight bag in his arms. He arrives home the next morning without any fish, drunk, tired and grumpy, he goes straight to bed?

Do you trust him or not?

Do you say anything?

Scenario 3: Your partner tells you he is attending a work event all weekend and you can only contact him by his mobile phone. One of the children are sick and in hospital, you want to do the right thing and let him know, also you wouldn't mind some moral support. You call his mobile numerous times and he doesn't answer.

Do you trust him or not?

What do you do?

Scenario 4: The doctor has told you, your child's stomach cramps are because of the food he is eating. The doctor gives you an eating plan of foods to avoid. You advise your partner of this and he states it's a lot of shit and it's your job to feed the kid so not his problem. You get called into work on a Saturday and have to leave your son with your partner, do you believe he will abide by the eating plan and look after your son?

Do you trust him or not?

Why?

My answer scenario 1 – No. Why? Because Family First - we are a family and he should want to spend time with his family. Occasionally going out is ok. For example, he plays tennis once a week on a Tuesday night. However, going out all the time is not, no matter what he is doing when he is out.

Especially when he is using the house money for his own entertainment, how are you going to feed the kids next week, what will you send them to school with? How are you going to pay your bills, when he is going out spending the house money all the time.

My answer scenario 2 – This situation happened to me, my ex-husband would go out with his mates fishing, not a problem. Until the night I realised why they were not catching any fish, because they were not going game fishing.

Worried I was over-reacting I contacted one of the guys, girlfriends and asked her how her partner was that morning. He was a good man and I knew if any of them were going to feel guilty he would. She told me he was amazing, he had driven to the bakery and made her a fresh breakfast in bed, she said, he had told her to relax whilst he cleaned her car inside and out. When I asked her if she knew they definitely went fishing last night. She said "As far as she knew. Why?" I explained to her my concerns, my intuitive feeling I was starting to listen to again. I explained, something felt funny, it didn't feel right. I explained, I think they went to the Casino. She said, "No way would he do that to her", so I left it.

My husband was still sleeping in bed whilst I did the house chores, I couldn't rid myself of that easy feeling.

My girlfriend rang me back ropable, she said you are right, they went to the Casino, she told me she was calling off the engagement because she would not be married to someone she couldn't trust. (She had self-worth and self-love)

NOTE: After a lot of work, he did feel guilty and was willing to do anything to make it up to her and through a lot of discussions. As far as I know he has never lied to her again and they are now married with 3 beautiful children.

I then woke my husband and asked him to tell me the truth and he skirted around for a while until he realised, I knew. Then he got angry, trying to turn it all around to be my fault, a trick he used often. I felt sick and was torn, at that moment I wanted to end the relationship because these events had happened more then once, but did I, No. I made excuses like what about the children? (I did not possess at that time enough self-love or self-worth)

My answer scenario 3 – This scenario also happened to me. No. My partner told me his boss was taking all the staff away for a team building weekend, I even helped him pack. Our daughter was really ill before he left, and whilst he was away, she ended up in hospital. I tried phoning his mobile and it continually reverted to message bank, I was worried about our daughter and gave him the benefit of the doubt, maybe his phone was dead and needed charging. I decided to call his boss, my partner did not know his boss had phoned me one morning from his mobile checking in as my partner had not arrived to work on time.

I innocently saved the number.

I phoned his boss who to my shock explained there was no work event this weekend. His boss was home with his family, he explained under his wife's instructions, there was no working on any weekends.

My insides died, he had lied again.

When he arrived home late Sunday night, he said he forgot to take his charger, reason for phone being dead and he blatantly denied not being at a work event.

He even went as far as giving examples of different situations. All were not true. This was the beginning of the end.

My answer scenario 4 – No. This happened to a client of mine and the child was rushed to hospital with major stomach cramps. Your partner has already expressed his opinion that the eating plan was rubbish, not even considering it could help your child.

Learning to trust yourself, your intuition can save your life and your children's. Remember if something doesn't feel right, it isn't.

No. 3 – HONESTY

Many relationships are built on lies, they start with innocent little white lies that grow into big black lies.

Some of us believe it is ok to lie to our partner. But what happens when you build your perception of white lie, upon white lie? Your relationship can find itself in a web of lies. Don't you want to be with someone you can be 100 percent honest with – and a partner who will be 100% honest with you. True freedom in a relationship comes from the power of honesty.

NOTE: Some people are compulsive liars which means they believe their own lies, they believe the reality they create and therefore can lie, continually with no remorse, some can even beat lie detector tests because they believe in what they are saying or have done to be true.

Answer the questions below, my answers are at the end of the questions.

Question 1 – Is it ok to tell a little while lie if asked what have you got me for my birthday or Christmas?

Question 2 – Is it ok to tell a little white lie about the new dress you saw on special and purchased?

Question 3 – Is it ok to lie about where you are going?

Question 4 – Is it ok to lie about where you spend your wages?

My answer question 1 – Yes, this is not an ongoing situation. You are protecting the person from finding out what their present is and teaching them how to be patient and wait until the special day. It's healthy, fun and pleasant you are not hurting anybody's feelings or emotions.

My answer question 2 – No, I understand in every relationship people do this but why? What fear do you have not to be honest with your partner about what you purchased? My reason being my ex-husband would purchase Snap on tools every week and never told me, remember he was also a gambler, and we lived off my money. His Snap on bill was massive and unfair on our family at the time.

A way to remedy this is to discuss openly with your partner, at what price do they wish to know what you spend your money on? It may be anything under $100 go for it, but anything over $100 needs to be discussed by both parties prior to purchase. (The amount is only used as a tool, you would discuss your own agreed amount depending on your family income)

My answer question 3 – Yes and No – If you are going to pick up a present or are organising a surprise then yes, but if you are sneaking out to gamble, have an affair or go against the respect and trust of your partner then No.

My answer question 4 – No, this scenario happened to a client of mine, her partner never had any money to contribute to bills and would lie about where his wages would disappear to, stating Child Support is taking all my money, bloody ex-wife etc. He would be paid on a Wednesday and there was no money on the Thursday. He has a massive Child Support debt now as he wasn't paying child support he was gambling and had she known sooner she may have been able to help him.

No 4 – COMMUNICATION

Open, honest communication is wonderful but very hard to do. There's a difference between talking at someone and talking to someone. A healthy conversation between two people does not result in raised voices or vicious emotional attacks. Communicate to each other with love and compassion and check your own ego at the door. Speak, listen, and really hear what each other is saying. Don't just wait for your turn to speak … hear your partner out.

Answer the scenarios below, my answers are at the end of the 3rd scenario.

Scenario 1 – Your partner comes home from being out all day and you ask the question "How was your day?".
He gets upset with you and yells at you "It's none of your business, you stupid bitch, where I have been or what I do!". You scream back "Of course it's my business, you dickhead, I'm your partner, what are you hiding?"
Is this open honest communication?
Write down how this scenario could be different?

Scenario 2 – Your husband comes home from work, angry and tells you, you have to attend a dinner with him on a certain date and time. You have nothing to wear, after giving birth you don't go out much. Excited to attend the dinner you ask if you could buy a new dress for the event. He starts ranting, throwing things around, "What do you think I am made of money? Surely you have some bloody dress you have bought without my knowledge in the cupboard? Are you so useless you can't even think for yourself?

You be quiet and continue making dinner with tears in your eyes.

Is this open honest communication?

Write down how this scenario could be different?

Scenario 3 – Your daughter asks if she can attend a party and you find out all the details and say yes. Your partner comes home and before you have time to tell him, your daughter being so excited shares her happy information that she is going to attend a party. Your partner goes off at her, yelling she is to young and she is not going. Upset and crying she runs up stairs to her bedroom hating the world. He gives you that pissed off glair and does not speak with you for the rest of the night.

Is this open honest communication?

Write down how this scenario could be different?

My answer scenario 1 – No this is not open, honest communication for a couple of reasons.

Firstly, voices are raised, and both are reacting to each other, not responding to each other.

Secondly, because each other calls the other names which is disrespectful.

In a healthy relationship this scenario, by responding instead of reacting to the situation, would sound something like:

You acknowledge him as you are walking towards him to give him a hug and a kiss hello, "How was your day?" (A healthy normal daily routine)

He responds with, "My day was so stressful, I am so happy to be home"; or

"My day was so stressful, I just need half an hour down time by myself"

The night continues with loving, happy energy.

My answer scenario 2 – No this is not open, honest communication for a few reasons.

Firstly, he tells you, you are going to this dinner and doesn't ask you.

Secondly, he raises his voice and wants to start an argument calling you names.

Thirdly, he has made you feel like you cannot speak your words.

In a healthy relationship this scenario, by responding and not reacting would sound something like:

Him: "Hi honey I'm home, I've had a stressful day and we have been asked to attend a work dinner, would you mind going with me?"

You respond "Hi sweetheart, sorry you had a stressful day. I would love to attend thank you for asking. After having the baby, I don't have anything to wear, I would need to buy a dress?"

Him: "Let's go out tomorrow night and pick something up. I know how hard is for you to shop with our baby by yourself!"

You: "That would be great"

My answer scenario 3 – No this is not open, honest communication for a couple of reasons.

Firstly, he reacted badly to the news yelling and becoming controlling.

Secondly, he does not address the situation with you, however, gives you the silent treatment like you have done something wrong.

In a healthy relationship this scenario, by responding and not reacting would sound something like:

Daughter: "Welcome home Dad, guess what I am going to a party this Saturday with all my friends!"

Dad: "Really love, has mum got all the details?"

Daughter: "Yes, she even has the phone numbers of all my friends attending the party and their parents phone numbers"

Dad: "Ok"

Daughter and father hug and the trust is being built.

Dad speaks with his wife "Hey love, Mary told me she is going to some party, I thought we were to always discuss such events?"

Mum, "I know sweetheart, she asked me at the beginning of the week, we have been so busy I didn't get a chance to discuss it with you. She needed an answer this afternoon, I tried to phone you, but your phone went to message bank, so I had to make a decision."

Dad, "I understand, this has been such a busy week, as long as we are still on the same page."

Mum: "Of course we are."

This outcome does not involve the daughter being yelled at, because the issue wasn't her, it was the parents being too busy to communicate. Very normal scenario that can be handled with loving, open, honest communication.

No 5 – CONNECTION

Your relationship should be your priority. This is your sacred place, your biggest support – your partner should have your back. They deserve to be our priority just as much as we deserve to be theirs, it must be both ways.

Make a point to connect with each other daily.

Even if you have to book a time when the kids are a sleep and you sit together and connect.

Above all else, enjoy life together, maybe a date night once a week or fortnight, no work, no phone, no children just the two of you.

It's far too easy to get caught up in our own careers or children. They tend to take priority these days, but the truth is your relationship should be your priority.

Don't miss out on your beautiful love story because your focused on earning more money or running around after the children.

Children do need our time, don't get me wrong, however so do our partners.

Dedicate real quality time to connect with your partner.

TOP TIP: Book a recurring date night, quality time with your partner, once a week, or once a fortnight, whatever suits the both of you.

You make time in your diary for work commitments, so make sure you mark this time off in your diary recurring weekly or fortnightly.

You need to make sure it is quality time, turn your phones off or on silent, book a baby sitter for the children, make sure on that one-night you put each other first and work does not get in the way.

Real quality time between the two of you.

This doesn't have to cost a lot of money, go to the movies, attend your favourite restaurant, or a drive and picnic.

When you master these five things, you will master your relationships.

It's time to stop settling for less than you deserve. It's time for you to embrace healthy relationships.

KNOW – you are worthy, and that real healthy relationships do exist.

Now ask yourself, does your current relationship have these 5 qualities?

If yes, you are blessed and congratulations

If no, ask yourself, can your current relationship obtain these qualities? If not, why not?

List what changes you believe need to be made in your current relationship for you to live in a healthy relationship?

MODULE SIX: BOUNDARIES for your Relationship

Boundaries and requirements somewhat go hand in hand. Let's discuss more aspects of healthy relationships between two people. They are also characterised by mutual respect, equality, trust, communication, and freedom.

Each person should feel they are allowed to be an individual within the relationship.

Both people grow independently of each other and together as a couple.

We all have the choice to set boundaries in our relationships and our boundaries are individual and personal.

This module is created to help you understand and set reasonable boundaries for yourself which will enhance your life. Boundaries are a part of self-love, self-worth and self-respect. When we love ourselves and know we are worthy and have respect for ourselves, we understand we make the choice on how we are treated. If we allow people to treat us badly, that is a choice. Setting stable boundaries for yourself is a must.

Write down a list what boundaries you currently have for your relationship?

How did you go? Do you know what your current boundaries are?

Here is a little guide to help you to understand boundaries and add to your boundary list:

1. Know this sad truth:

   ### NO boundaries = little or no self-esteem

2. Work out what your core values are?
3. Understand you cannot change your partner, you can only change yourself.
4. Decide the consequences ahead of time.
5. Let your behaviour, not your words, speak for you.
6. Say what you mean and mean what you say.

It is very important to set clear personal boundaries, to ensure your relationships are mutually supportive, respectful and caring.

Boundaries are a measure of self-esteem

A healthy self-esteem will produce boundaries which show you deserve to be treated well.

I believe there are different sets of boundaries, the first set I would like to discuss is **"I will leave Boundaries",** this means that if any event below occurs in your relationship, you will not hesitate to leave because your partner has crossed one or more of your boundaries and has completely disrespected you. Being we are emotional beings, we may have different leaving boundaries. I provide you with a list of my leaving boundaries to use, all you need to do is circle agree/disagree for you.

Your partner hits or physically abuses you? **Agree/Disagree**

Your partner has an affair? **Agree/Disagree**

Your partner gambles your family money away?

Agree/Disagree

Your partner abuses your children? **Agree/Disagree**

Your partner emotionally abuses you on an ongoing basis?

Agree/Disagree

Your partner rapes or sexually abuses you? **Agree/Disagree**

All the above are my "I will leave Boundaries" no exception and my current husband is aware of them and the consequence should he cross any of them. I will leave and for us it is visa-versa.

After escaping my domestic violence relationships, I realised I did not have a healthy self-respect or self-worth. I sat down and wrote out what I required in a relationship, what my reasonable boundaries where and what the consequences would be if they were not adhered to.

I had to find out where my line in the sand was.

When I met my current husband, I walked into the relationship with my bag full of reasonable requirements and knew my leaving Boundaries.

We spoke about our mutual "leaving Boundaries" however because I respected myself, my actions spoke louder than any words in relation to all my normal boundaries.

My current husband has always respected me, because I respect myself and I respect him.

However, working as a Relationship Therapist, I understand that some couples want to work on their relationships and some of my "leaving Boundaries" do not apply to them.

For example - I help people reconnect after an affair;

or help them build their self-worth and self-esteem to conquer ongoing emotional abuse;

or I help couples create boundaries when one is a gambler and tools to reconnect as a couple;

or I help couples create boundaries when one takes drugs and/or alcohol and provide tools to help them reconnect as a couple.

I do not judge anyone, just because the above are my "leaving Boundaries", they do not all have to be yours.

You may have other "leaving Boundaries" that you would like to list relative to you.

Remember boundaries leaving or normal are a self-choice, not a discussion with a partner, but your own choice.

I am proud to advise that I have helped many couples over the years reconnect in those situations, it isn't easy, and it takes a lot of patience and time. It takes both parties really wanting to acknowledge the mistakes, take the time, learn the art of forgiveness and really let go of their emotional attachment to that boundary to move forward.

It is achievable, you can't work through this alone and need to contact a Relationship Therapist or Family Counsellor. You can find someone to help you in module 8 of this course.

Now other boundaries for your relationship can be set to ensure you create a healthy relationship.

Below I will explain more healthy relationship points and provide you the opportunity to address if they work for you or not.

No. 1 – COMMUNICATION

Do you both really listen to each other? Write yes or no and then write an example when you have or haven't been able to.

Can you speak openly about what is important to you with your partner? Write yes or no and then write an example when you have or haven't been able to.

Can you speak openly and honestly and work out your disagreements? Write yes or no and then write an example when you have or haven't been able to.

As referred to in *Module 5, Requirements*, communication is a major requirement for a healthy relationship.
What are your boundaries when it comes to communication?
An example: One of my communication boundaries is not to be called names or viciously yelled at.

No. 2 - TRUST

Do you feel safe around each other? Write yes or no and then write an example when you have or haven't felt safe.

Are you honest with each other? Write yes or no and then write an example when you have or haven't been honest.

Do you believe each other? Write yes or no and then write an example when you have or haven't believed in each other.

As referred to in *Module 5, Requirements,* trust is a major requirement for a healthy relationship.

What are your boundaries when it comes to trust?

My example: Trust to me is the most important part of a
healthy relationship.

I need to feel safe with my partner.

I will speak with my partner about a situation when my
intuition is crying out something is wrong and try and work
through the situation with him.

However, if he lies or is deceitful, he plants that seed of doubt
which is extremely difficult for me to work past.

No 3 – Freedom

**Can you make decisions for yourself within your
relationship?** Write yes or no and then write an example
when you have or haven't been able to make decisions.

Are you concerned about your partners reaction if you make a decision for yourself? Write yes or no and then write an example when you have been concerned.

Can you go out if you chose to with the girls without him? Write yes or no and then write an example when you have or haven't been able to go out with the girls.

Can you visit your family and friends without him? Write yes or no and then write an example when you have or haven't been able to visit your family or friends without him. What does he do?

What are your boundaries when it comes to freedom?

My example: My boundary for freedom, is having the freedom to be able to visit who I want, when I want without the fear of reprisal. My husband trust's me and in our relationship, unlike the Devil who would not allow me to see family or friends by myself. The Devil allowed me to go to work and come home directly after work finished, he timed me and would ring the home phone, if he wasn't home. If I didn't answer, I would be punished when he returned.

No. 4 – RESPECT

Are you both being treated respectfully by the other?

Write Yes or No and reasons for your answer.

What are your boundaries when it comes to respect?
My example: Being respected in a relationship is extremely important. I am a very spiritual person, my husband not so much. He doesn't put me down or berate me for my beliefs, he acknowledges we are different and even though he doesn't fully understand, he respects me.

No. 5 – EQUALITY
Is your relationship a balance of give and take? Write a list of what you both contribute to your relationship. Chores, children, finances etc

Do you view each other as equals? Write Yes or No and why?

What are your boundaries when it comes to Equality?

My example: My husband does not expect me to do all of the housework and be his slave. We work together in our relationship as equal partners. We both work outside the home and we share the responsibilities inside the home.

Finding out what boundaries work for you can be time consuming, especially if you are living in a domestic violence relationship.

I recommend taking your time and adding to your list as disrespectful situations arise, remembering all relationships are different and require different boundaries.

For example, your partner may never call you names, this does not mean that boundary does not exist. It means you have found someone that works within your boundaries.

Most importantly remember that your boundaries, are your boundaries. In a healthy relationship both parties will have their own set of boundaries.

TIP

DO NOT TRY AND PLACE YOUR NEW BOUNDARIES ON YOUR CURRENT PARTNER IF HE/SHE IS ABUSIVE.

This will take time to integrate into your current relationship.

If you feel you are in danger, phone the Police, immediately.

If you are realising you are residing in a domestic violence relationship and not in danger, it is most beneficial for you to create an action plan to leave. I refer to COURSE 2, Escaping Domestic Violence, it has step by step tools in detail to help you create your action plan to leave.

NOTE: BOUNDARIES AND CONSEQUENCES are provided in this course to provide you with the knowledge of what type of relationship you are living in, healthy or unhealthy. And tools to help you create some if you have none.

Once you have your updated list of your boundaries, the next step is to write down what the consequences to those boundaries are?

Consequences are personal. In a healthy relationship they can be easy.

Examples: 1 Your partner ignores you at a party, this is not a leaving boundary, however the feeling of being disrespected arises.

Consequence: In a healthy relationship you would speak with him about how his actions made you feel and if that is how he would like to act, you are not the right partner for him. Providing him with a choice that is totally his and respecting yourself.

2 You realise your partner is drinking too much and may be an alcoholic. His personality changes in a negative way when he drinks, he becomes abusive and unkind.

Consequence (a) you speak with your partner about how his drinking is affecting the relationship, that you love him and don't want the relationship to end. You request that he seeks help to stop the drinking eg: attend "Alcoholics Anonymous" and you would go with him. He agrees.

(b) If your partner doesn't want to acknowledge the issue and it is really affecting your relationship, the next consequence could be you leave, as this relationship will only get worse.

What consequences will you state for your boundaries?

Write the boundary and next to it a consequence?

MODULE SEVEN:
Additional Tools

Are you feeling overwhelmed? Cannot think straight? Take time out and try and use some of the tools that helped me.

I provide you with different tools in this module to help you calm your mind and change your mindset. You can start by using one, two or all three.

I started slowly, worked on affirmations until I was comfortable and then began my grateful "gratitude" journal which I still do today and then the meditation.

Did you know what you think, you create? For example: when you don't feel you are worthy, you are not worthy, and people treat you as if you are not worthy.

Know you are worthy.

1. Meditation
2. Affirmations
3. Grateful "Gratitude" Journal

Meditation

Shedding Unnecessary Baggage

Imagine, for a moment, you are about to begin a new exciting journey.

What do you want to let go of? Eg: Negativity, avoidance, sadness, social awkwardness, drugs, alcohol, negative relationships, abusive relationships, excess weight just to name a few. Write your list below?

What has become too burdensome or unnecessary on your journey?

At some point, it becomes apparent that you have accumulated far too much emotional baggage. You've been lugging it around for far too long and life feels heavy. It's time to unload—drop a few thousand dead leaves and prune a couple hundred branches.

Like nature, you need to clear out the thick brush and rid yourself of things you've been afraid to let go of. It's time to abandon the rules of society that seek to convince you it's not acceptable to speak your truth—to quiet that voice that convinces you to stay uncomfortably comfortable right where you are.

Now is a good time to shed anything that binds you to your indignant and stubborn ways of sabotaging your dreams. Without letting go, there can be no new growth.

Guided Meditation

Retreat inward, light a candle, and see what emotional situations need clearing.

Try this guided meditation to tune in, listen, and reflect on where you are in your life.

1. Find a comfortable seat on your couch, chair, or in your favourite place in nature. If you prefer lie down facing directly towards the ceiling, sky depending on where you are.

2. Settle into your body by connecting with your breath—slowly inhaling through your nose for 5 counts, slowly exhaling through your mouth for 5 counts. Close your eyes and notice how your body and mind begin to soften and relax, and you feel a tingling feeling.

3. Visualize a scene from nature: the reds, browns, darker greens, and yellows of the terrain around you, a cool breeze blowing, and the dryness of the brush, branches, and earth. Or sitting on the beach, with the wind blowing and the waves thumping.

4. Now, imagine that your body, your breath, your emotions, and your mind are an extension of nature. Perhaps you see yourself as a tall oak tree, the mist rising off a lake at dawn, or you're simply basking in the late afternoon sunset or the golden glow of the moon.

5. Be aware that you are about to embark on an inward journey. As you prepare to rest and prepare for the budding of a new you, dare yourself to dream of:

   o the person you would like to be

   o the relationship you would like to have

   o activities you want to do

   o the environment you thrive in most

   o the lifestyle you want to have when you wake up from your deep sleep

Let your imagination run wild and allow yourself to see what you would see, to hear what you would hear, and to feel what you would feel if your dream came true.

6. Next, notice an area of your life where there is some heaviness—a burden or an unnecessary load. Perhaps your baggage is within the area of your intimate relationship, your career, your health and fitness, or family.

   Let yourself see where there is an over-accumulation of emotional upset, mental challenges, or spiritual disconnect.

7. Next, reconnect with your dream of what your life could look like, feel like, and sound like once you are free of the burdensome weight you have been carrying. What would you be doing then that is different from how you are living now?

   o How would your relationships begin to thrive?

   o How would your energy levels and mental clarity be propelling you toward your goals?

   o Create an internal representation (a visual image, a feeling, or a sound) of how you, your life, and your surroundings could be different.

8. As you bask in your picture of how things could be, ask yourself what qualities you would need to embrace to be

the type of person who could powerfully catapult yourself from beneath the weight of what you now carry to the new you that awaits?

- o Do you need to have more compassion toward yourself or others?

- o Do you need to listen more attentively without the need to fix things or justify your position?

- o Do you need to cultivate more strength, so you can set and maintain your boundaries?

- o Do you need to be more honest and find a loving yet direct way to speak your truth?

- o What characteristics would be most beneficial to acquire so that you can begin to take your next steps?

9. Now, envisioning the traits or characteristics that are empowering you to create change, ask yourself "what action steps do I need to take to feel inspired and motivated to charge powerfully forward?"

- o What emotions, beliefs, or behaviours do I need to let go of, so that I can stop being a victim and become the person I am meant to be?"

Ask your heart for guidance rather than your intellect and allow yourself to hear what practice you need to cultivate or what action you need to take to change your inner-outer world to clear a path for your next journey.

10.   When you are ready, take a few slow, deep breaths and open your eyes. Now is the time to make notes about whatever came up for you during the guided meditation.

Write down:

- **How you want to be living your life**

- **What needs to be cleared out**

- **What qualities or characteristics you need to embrace**

- ○ **What specific action steps you need to take, including something you can do today**

Go do that thing today. Tomorrow, do the next thing, and so on.

This will help you take charge of your life. It's a process of letting go of anything that isn't you—toxic relationships, limiting beliefs, and obstacles that prevent you from living your dream.

It allows you to take responsibility for every choice you make and every action you take (or don't take).

Whenever you begin a new path, anything you haven't cleared out or brought to completion will follow you onto the new path, so now is the time to let go of anything you need to leave commence your new life.

Approach your life with anticipation, preparation, and excitement. Observe its energy and watch as it cyclically moves through its phases—transitioning from one moment to the next, sometimes intensely and sometimes gently.

Nature moves slowly and deliberately toward harmony and sustainability. It intrinsically knows what it needs to do and simply does it.

You can learn a lot by tuning into this process in your own life. That is only if you slow down enough and pay close attention.

Understand that you can change your views, even whilst still living in your unhealthy relationship.

If this meditation is to difficult to do alone, I suggest googling "YouTube" for "Guided Meditations to Release the Past, Release Negativity, Build Self-Love" they are free and I suggest when you find the one you like for you, take the time out to listen to it every-day.

Affirmations

I provide you with some healthy affirmations that I suggest you say or write down daily. I suggest you pick 5 affirmations that resonate with you and each day when you wake up write them down or say them.

Saying or writing affirmations on a daily basis in the morning helps you to change your thought processes and start the day with positive energy.

Let me get started:

- I am worthy.
- I am beautiful.
- I am open for real unconditional love.
- I claim my power and move beyond all limitations.
- I welcome miracles into my life.
- Only good can come to me.
- Wellness is the natural state of the body. I am in perfect health.
- I know that old negative patterns no longer limit me. I let them go with ease.
- I am greeted with love wherever I go.
- I attract only healthy relationships. I am always treated well.
- I do not have to prove myself to anyone.
- I release all drama from my life.
- I balance my life between work, rest and play.
- I spend time with positive energetic people.

- I release all negative thoughts of past and all worries about the future.
- I forgive everyone in my past for all perceived wrongs. I release them with love.
- Negativity has no part in my life.
- My life gets better all the time.
- It is safe for me to speak up for myself.
- Perfect health is my divine right and I claim it now.
- My income is constantly increasing.
- Love flows through my body, healing all dis-ease.

This was extremely hard for me to do initially, but I did not give up. Every day for 28 days (it is said it takes 21 days to change a behaviour) I wrote the same 5 affirmations.
Then I chose a different 5 affirmations and repeated the cycle.
The mind is a wonderful tool and my world did change.
So even if you don't believe it now, all I suggest is you give it a go.

Write down below the 5 affirmations that resonate with you today? Then everyday in a book that is just for you, write them down.

-
-
-
-
-

Grateful Journal

Writing a grateful journal when you don't feel grateful for anything in your life right now, is the perfect time to start. This was easy for me and like I said above I still have a Grateful Journal today.

All you do is write down daily, three things you are grateful for:
For example:
I am grateful for the air I breath.
I am grateful for my beautiful daughter.
I am grateful for my inner strength.

The next day and each day after you write down three different things you are grateful for, it can be anything at all, after all it is what you are grateful for.
When you start, I recommend you write the journal for at least two months.

MODULE EIGHT:
Helpful Services

NOTE: I have not listed all service providers that may be able to assist you. If none of the below can help or you reside outside Australia (current September 2018), I suggest google Domestic Violence providers or Police in your area and contact them.

If in immediate danger, call the **Police** in your country
Australia 000
America 911
England 999

Centrelink – Can help you with obtaining payments, etc, to leave an abusive relationship-
https://www.humanservices.gov.au/customer/subjects/family-and-domestic-violence

1800 RESPECT - National Sex Assault, Domestic Family Violence Counselling Service
https://www.1800respect.org.au
Phone number 1800 737 732

Lifeline 24/7 – phone 131114
https://www.lifeline.org.au

Relationship Resolutions – phone 0426 218869
https://www.relationshipresolutions.com.au

Women's Legal Services Queensland – phone 1800 957 957
www.wlsq.org.au

Mens Helpline 24/7 – phone 1300 78 99 78
http://www.mensline.org.au

Kids Helpline 24/7 – phone 1800 55 1800
https://kidshelpline.com.au

Child Abuse Protection Services – Phone 02 9716 8000
http://www.childabuseprevention.com.au

Another Closet for LGBTIQ Lesbian, Gay, Bisexual, Transgender, Intersex and Queer People Phone: 1800 65 64 63
http://www.anothercloset.com.au

White Ribbon Australia – Phone - 02 9045 8444
https://www.whiteribbon.org.au/find-help

Homelessness Australia – Phone - 02 6247 7744
http://www.homelessnessaustralia.org.au

Family Relationships
http://www.familyrelationships.gov.au

Alcoholics Anonymous – Phone – 1300 222 222
http://www.aa.org.au

Family Drug Support Australia – Phone – 1300 368 186
http://www.fds.org.au

Gamblers Anonymous – check website for your state's contact details
http://gaaustralia.org.au

If you are abusing, and want to stop, check out:
Domestic Violence Prevention Centre – After hours support 1800 811 811 or check out their website below for further information: -

http://www.domesticviolence.com.au/pages/getting-help-for-abusive-behaviours.php

Daisy is an app that connects you to services in your state and local area. Use Daisy to create a list of favourite services for easy reference such as legal, housing, finance, and children's services. https://www.1800respect.org.au/daisy

You can also search the internet with Daisy and understand what to expect when contacting a service.

Your family members and friends can download Daisy to gather information and provide you with support.

Penda is an app from the Women's Legal Service that helps with financial abuse

Download *Daisy* and or *Penda* from Google Play or App Store.

If you live in America, look into Robin McGraw's app for help save you from domestic violence
https://www.drphil.com/show-pages/14016_aspirenewsapp/

MODULE NINE:
Conclusion

Wow, how do you feel? I know I ask this question nearly at the beginning of each module, this is because I care and if you ever have attended or do attend one of my workshops, you would or will understand. My life purpose is to help you understand there is life outside of abuse, that healthy happy relationships do exist and to help you find your inner self-love.

Are you living in a healthy or unhealthy relationship?

Are you living in domestic violence and fear for your life?

STOP right now and immediately call the Police in your country

Remember: If you are living in domestic violence and don't want to leave, be kind to yourself, be smart, get yourself together.

If you are taking drugs or drinking too much alcohol, to either fit in or make the pain go away, STOP especially if you have children.

I realise it is not that easy to just stop, however try to start reducing your intake. Get your life back for you, realise not only does your partner have a hold on you and keeps you in a bad place, so do the drugs and alcohol.

Ask for help, it is here for you, refer to Module 8 for assistance if you are unsure where to start.

Give yourself the best chance you can, keep a clear mind while you work out your feelings and gain your inner strength. Sometimes the process to happiness takes a long time, just know it is worth it.

You now have the information to make an informed choice. Remembering there are always consequences to our choices.

Moving forward, you now know you have choices and have more knowledge now, to make informed choices.

Possible choice suggestions no 1:
Your relationship may be unhealthy, but not dangerous and it only has a few glitches, when those glitches are worked on your relationship could be healthy again.
For you, I hope your partner will come to the party and work through this course with you and changes may be possible.
If he doesn't want to or that doesn't work, I suggest finding a relationship therapist you can work with in your area, if there are none, find one that works online or over the phone they are out there, one for example is
www.relationshipresolutions.com.au They will help you to tweak your relationship to happiness and sometimes learning how to love yourself, and work on yourself is all you need to change the relationship. When we change how we react or respond to situations, our partners tend to change as well.

Obviously, there are exceptions however sometimes it can be
all the tweaking that is required.

Possible choice suggestion no. 2

You can stay in an unhealthy relationship and hope for the best, hope he/she will change, will realise how much you love them, how much you do for them, how much you put up with and hope that miracle happens when they may learn unconditional love for you, or

You can start to work on your action plan to leave, this does not mean you are leaving immediately, you are just getting prepared, in case you need to leave. This will take patience and time, depending on the severity of abuse in your relationship.

I am not going anywhere, I wouldn't dream of leaving you feeling alone, with your new insight and information. I do understand how hard it is to make that decision to leave, even when we have confirmed we are living in an unhappy, unhealthy or domestic violence relationship.

If you have children and are thinking it isn't fair on them to take them away from the other parent, this is just an excuse, a lie we tell ourselves.

Let me share with you a potential scenario, our daughters are learning how to be treated by their future partner, the cycle of abuse WILL continue, she will accept abuse into her life, because you allow it in yours and because little girls love their dads and want to grow up and marry someone like daddy.

It doesn't matter if she thinks that, we learn by our environment and she is being taught love = abuse.

And our sons may grow up to be abusers themselves and hurt women or worse as he grows older, all his pent-up anger for not being protected and not being able to protect you when he was younger. Seeing you being hurt by his dad, all that anger finally erupts and he kills his dad. His future, gaol for the rest of his life.

Do you want that for your children?

Don't you love them more then you love him?

Afterall they can't protect themselves.

It is NOT fair on the children for you to stay, you need to protect your children, they should grow up feeling safe not unsafe, scared and/or abused.

Possible Choice suggestion no. 3

You have made the choice to leave. You want to start working on your action plan to leave as soon as possible. You don't rock the boat, you have realised you are not in love with your partner and that he/she has been controlling you, because somewhere, back in time, you made the choice to allow him to treat you this way and it has now become the norm. You realise you are not crazy and feel like a weight has been taken off your shoulders and you realise you are living in a toxic relationship that you need to get out of.

So, I suggest the following:

If you are totally shocked and scared, fearful for your life, are in danger now, call the Police in your country immediately.

Do not wait, your life and your children's lives are more important than anything else. Everything else can be worked out later and there is help for you.

If you are unsure, confused and need to talk to someone check module 8 for an organisation near you.

If you reside in Australia, you could also call 1800Respect.

If you are thinking of leaving or ready to leave and would like some tools that I utilised when I left, look up **Course 2 – Escaping Domestic Violence, Action Plan,** you can start to work on building your action plan to leave, this does not mean you are leaving immediately, but just in case or the faster you work through the course the faster you can leave.

This course was created with the tools I utilised to leave all those years ago and updated tools that will work in today's world in relation to leaving your abusive relationship as safely as possible. You can purchase this course at www.melaniesurvivor.com

The tools provided in this course can be utilised by anyone who is leaving an unhealthy or domestic violence relationship.

If you need empowerment or courage, I suggest if you haven't had the opportunity to read my book, **_"Surviving the Devil, Escaping Domestic Violence"_**, you can purchase the book at my webpage www.melaniesurvivor.com as explained earlier, it provides my personal journey of escaping domestic violence, the ups and downs, and six other peoples journeys on how they escaped and where they are now, it also provides the basic tools to leaving a domestic violence relationship.

I know you may not feel it right now. I do remember that feeling when I first realized I was living in abuse and it was soul destroying.

I always thought the relationship issues were my fault, believe me they weren't.

I needed to be smart, I didn't tell the abuser how I was feeling or what my plans where, life had to go on just the way it was. I never gave a hint I was planning on leaving.

You need to be smart, you don't say anything to your abuser, life must go on as normal, so he/she is unaware until you are out safely.

I never knew the strength I had once I started the process. I didn't realise I had become a chameleon, he found me the first few times, the last time though, he had no idea, I disappeared.

I wish you every happiness and success in moving forward and creating the healthy relationship that you and if you have children, they deserve.

P.S. Keep up to date with upcoming seminars, events, releases on Facebook at: www.facebook.com/melaniesurvivor

PRODUCTS & SERVICES

Melanie Survivor is a relationship expert not only by her qualifications, she holds a Diploma in Relationship Education/Counselling, Diploma in Law and Business Management, Certificate IV in Training and Assessment, Advanced counselling skills working with persons with Intellectual and Learning Disabilities, Cross Cultural Trainer, Money and You Graduate Certificate, Master Life Coaching Certificate, Conflict Resolution, Working with difficult candidates, Team Building, Assistant and Executive Management Training.

However, her true expertise has come from working with families, couples, singles and children from all walks of life with their relationship issues. She exudes real empathy as she has walked similar paths in her own life experiences.

She broke the cycle of abuse within herself, and so changed the lives of herself and her children.

Mel understands it doesn't matter if you are male or female, you must love yourself, build your self-worth, self-confidence and self-respect, clean up your emotional backyard and learn what your relationship requirements are, before you will find and live in an amazing relationship.

Her passion and empathy to help others has led to her creating products and services to help you traverse through your relationship issues, by providing you with tools to lead a loving, honest, relationship. These are the same tools and questions she knows would have made her journey a lot easier.

The courses are written in easy to follow modules, self- paced and easy to access on-line at www.melaniesurvivor.com

    Course 2 Escaping Domestic Violence – Action Plan
    Course 3 Women First
    Course 4 Legal Toolbox for Separation/Divorce
    Course 5 Cleaning up your Backyard

Course 6 Budgeting to get ahead
Course 7 Pre-marriage counselling
Course 8 Parenting/Co-Parenting the Children
Course 9 Dating in Today's World
Course 10 Living in a Happy Step Family

Or you can book Mel to run a tailored exclusive course for your organisation or speak at your seminar as a key speaker, she is a woman of integrity, she is real, and always exudes her positive outlook on life.
NOTE: Mel gives **20%** to charity with every purchase.

9 780648 516002